Write Starts

101 Writing Prompts for Math

Margaret E. McIntosh

Roni Jo Draper

Dale Seymour Publications®

Project Editor: Mali Apple
Production/Manufacturing Director: Janet Yearian
Production/Manufacturing Coordinator: Shannon Miller
Design Manager: John F. Kelly
Composition: Andrea Reider
Cover and Illustrations: Rachel Gage

ISBN 0-86651-953-X
Printed in the United States of America
6 7 8 9 10 11 12   06 05 04 03

1-800-321-3106
www.pearsonlearning.com

Contents

About *Write Starts*

Whether you are experimenting with using writing in your mathematics classes or are already committed to having your students write, we believe you will enjoy the ideas in *Write Starts: 101 Writing Prompts for Math.* The writing prompts in this collection have all been used successfully by many teachers.

The writing prompts are easy and convenient to use. They are grouped into twelve sections that address key areas of concern; use them in any order that fits your lesson plan. There are two prompts on each page, which may be made into transparencies or photocopied for individual student use. The front and back of a half page will usually give students plenty of room to respond, but you can give them a full page by covering the other prompt while you photocopy.

Many of the prompts reinforce the positive aspects of math. Too many students have only ever heard the negative side and have had that reinforced. We want to accentuate the positive, both verbally and in writing.

Communicating Mathematically

You are probably already aware of the power of using writing in conjunction with mathematics. The National Council of Teachers of Mathematics' Curriculum and Evaluation Standards for School Mathematics (NCTM 1989) puts forth five general goals for students:

1. that they learn to value mathematics

2 that they become confident in their ability to do mathematics

3. that they become mathematical problem solvers

4. that they learn to communicate mathematically

5. that they learn to reason mathematically (p. 5)

The fourth goal—learning to communicate mathematically—concerns the development of a student's power to use the signs, symbols, and terms of mathematics. The use of the language of mathematics becomes natural when students have an opportunity to read, write, and discuss ideas within the context of problem situations. "As students communicate their ideas, they learn to clarify, refine, and consolidate their thinking" (p. 6).

The goal of having students learn to communicate mathematically has led educators to include writing as part of the mathematics curriculum. Teachers who use the writing-process model for structuring writing experiences believe that the writing process involves five stages:

1. prewriting

2. composing (or drafting)

3. revising

4. editing (or proofreading)

5. publishing (or sharing)

Students will probably not go through all five stages when responding to the writing prompts in *Write Starts.* For example, they may or may not do prewriting. They will compose their writing, and then—depending on the purpose of the prompt—they may share their writing with others, post it on a bulletin board, or turn it in to be read by the teacher.

Geeslin (1977) points out that written explanations of mathematical concepts have several advantages over discussion, including

- simultaneous student participation
- availability of what students have written for further, closer examination by the teacher
- encouragement to be more precise in writing than in verbal expression
- availability of the written work for later inspection and discussion between teacher and student

The main purpose of the writing prompts in *Write Starts* is for students *to reflect on what they are learning* and *to learn while they are reflecting on what they are learning.*

Introducing Writing Prompts in Your Mathematics Class

When you introduce *Write Starts* writing prompts to your students, there will probably be some resistance. Unless your students came from a mathematics class in which writing was an integral part of the curriculum, they are likely to inform you that "this is math class—not English class." They will probably not understand the relevance of writing in math class the first time you give them an assignment; don't be surprised if they turn in hastily written, poorly conceived responses. Following is a typical introduction of *Write Starts* in a math class.

Teacher Today we are going to start something new. I'd like you to use the last few minutes of class to respond to this statement: "To solve this problem, I had to. . ." As you solve problem number 13 on page 245, think about all the steps you take, and tell me about them in writing. Use complete sentences, paragraphs, and correct punctuation—all the things good writing includes.

Student   Hey, this isn't *English* class. Why do we have to write in here?

Teacher   You're right. This is a math class. However, to show me that you understand what you're learning, I'd like you to explain it in writing.

Student   How long does it have to be?

Teacher   Long enough to tell me everything. There are reasons behind every step you take to solve this problem. I want you to tell me what each step is and why you chose it. When you have done that, you will be done.

Student   How much is this worth?

Teacher   I won't be grading this on whether it is wrong or right, but on whether you put an honest effort into your response. These writing exercises will be part of your participation grade for this class.

Student   I'm not going to have time to copy this over and fix my spelling. Can't I just take it home and do it on my computer?

Teacher   This is just first-draft writing. I'm just looking for ideas, and I'm not going to spend a lot of time marking off for spelling and grammar errors. Of course, I expect you to use grammar and spelling skills to the best of your ability.

Student   I'm done. I finished problem 13 on page 245.

The teacher reads the student's response. The student has finished the problem, but has written nothing about his reasoning.

Teacher   You did a great job solving the problem, but I need you to explain *how you knew how* to solve the problem. Sometimes you can work through a problem without understanding the steps or how they are connected. I want you to show me that you really understand how and why your solution works. If you can do this, it will be much easier for you to understand new information in upcoming lessons.

If you assign writing frequently and show your students that you are committed to making writing an integral part of their mathematics experience, they will soon adopt your attitude and commitment.

Assigning Prompts

Writing prompts are most effective if you assign them several times a week. Vary the presentation of the prompts so they do not become routine or monotonous.

- When you are looking for specific information about students' learning or attitudes, or when you have planned an activity around a specific writing prompt, give all students the same writing prompt to complete.
- Sometime you will want to offer students a choice of two or three prompts. Students will often give a more thoughtful response to a topic they have selected.

- You may want to make certain prompts available for students to use regardless of whether you have assigned them. You can designate a special place in your room where students know they will find copies of the prompts. Students are sometimes comfortable voicing a particular question or concern in writing, though they may never bring it up in class.
- You can keep copies of several prompts on hand to distribute when you have extra time at the end of a period.
- You may want to have students designate a section of their notebooks for writing questions, comments, and other thoughts they have about what they are learning. They could keep copies of writing prompts that you want accessible to them in their notebooks.

You can use the prompts in *Write Starts* in your classroom in several ways.

To open a lesson

When students enter your class, they may need help getting focused on mathematics. You can ask them to pick up a writing prompt as they walk into class (or to read a prompt that you display on the overhead). While you take roll, answer individual questions, or get stragglers out the door from your previous class, students can spend a few minutes responding to the prompt. When you start class, your students will already be thinking about mathematics.

To wrap up a lesson

Providing closure for lessons is an important part of good instruction because it allows students to take a few moments to reflect on what they have learned and to pull together information. When a few minutes remain in class and you want to continue the learning experience up until the bell, you can assign a writing prompt. A prompt that asks students to explain what they have learned or to connect what they have learned with another experience is ideal for providing lesson closure.

To evaluate students' learning

The prompts in *Write Starts* can provide feedback about how well your students understood the day's lesson. After reading the class's responses to a prompt, it may be clear that several students did not understand a concept you presented. You can modify your instruction for the next lesson to get students back on track.

To compel students to articulate their thinking

Students often say they understand something, but are unable to explain it. Having students explain their thinking *in writing* compels them to really think about a concept and their understanding of it. Also, once they begin to write, students can re-examine their thought processes in a way that they are unable to do in their heads.

To communicate individually with students

Most of us do not feel we have enough time to connect with our students individually. *Write Starts* writing prompts provide an opportunity for you to have mini-conversations with your students. Although it is not necessary to respond to every writing prompt, you can write back and forth with a student when you want to have an exchange of information and ideas on a particular issue.

To assess students' attitudes and biases

Too often, students erect barriers to their learning based on what they *think* mathematics is about. The writing prompts in Section 1, Assessing Attitudes and Stereotypes, will help you directly assess your students' attitudes toward mathematics and give you an opportunity to acknowledge their attitudes individually or through class discussion.

To examine students' study strategies and skills

Many of the prompts in *Write Starts* encourage students to evaluate their study skills. Student are asked to explain errors they made on their homework or to discuss the ways in which they study or take notes. This allows both you and your students to identify study skills that need improvement.

Showing Your Commitment

If you show your students that you believe writing plays an important part in learning, they are more likely to adopt a positive attitude. There are a number of ways you can let your students know that you are committed to the practice of writing in math class.

You can write along with your students. When students are reflecting on their learning, on stereotypes they hold, or on how they should do something, you can reflect with them. This sends a powerful message that you value the process enough to take part in it.

Do not accept partial, ill-conceived, or no-effort answers—just as you would not accept poor work in other areas of mathematics. We do not believe in grading the responses per se, but, since students often evaluate the value of a task based on whether it is "worth" something, we do suggest giving participation points or daily grade points.

The writing activities do not have to take a great deal of class time or grading time. You can often collect responses as students exit class and read them quickly to get an idea about how the day's lesson went. Sometimes you may want students to place their responses in their notebooks for you to review when you conduct notebook checks. Other times you may find it worthwhile to respond to what students have written before they return to class the next day.

Students need to know you are reading their writing assignments. Responding to what they have written lets them know you care about what they think. We suggest that however you respond, you do so positively. Students are more likely to accept your comments and suggestions, and it gives them one more positive connection to mathematics.

SECTION

1

Assessing Attitudes and Stereotypes

All teachers know that a student's attitude often determines what he or she will learn. Responses to the prompts in this section—and in a subsequent discussion, should you choose to have one—can provide insight into your students' attitudes and stereotypes about mathematics. After reading their responses, you can address negative attitudes and support positive ones.

Use the prompts in this section throughout the year at regular intervals. You may choose to have your students keep their responses in their portfolios to demonstrate their growth in their understanding of mathematics.

Prompt 1a   *What does a mathematician look like?*

Prompt 1 has two parts. They are intended to be used together, on consecutive days. On the first day, students describe what they think a mathematician looks like. They may add drawings to their written ideas if they like. Collect and read their responses, without comment, to see what stereotypes they hold about mathematicians. Ask students to bring in a picture of themselves for the follow-up activity.

Prompt 1b   *What does a mathematician look like?*

A day or two later, give students this prompt, with the directions that they attach their own picture in the space along with their answer and describe *themselves* as mathematicians. Make the case that mathematicians don't look any different from anyone else; there are no distinguishing features that allow one to determine who is— and who isn't—a mathematician. This year, in your class, *everyone* will be a mathematician. You might want to post students' descriptions on a bulletin board entitled, "Mathematicians in Our Midst."

Prompt 2   *Hmm . . . How does a mathematician think?*

Along with Prompt 1, this prompt will help flush out the stereotypes your students have about mathematicians. You will be able to see whether your students believe that a mathematician thinks differently or has a different kind of brain. After having students write their ideas, you may want to hold a brief classroom discussion on this topic (if students complete this prompt at the end of a class period, you can begin the next day by presenting some of their ideas for discussion).

Prompt 3   *When will we ever use this stuff?*

This oft-heard question is one that needs to be addressed. We have found that often students really *do* know when they will use "this stuff," but act as though they do not. This prompt gives you the chance to ask *them* the question before they ask *you.*

Prompt 4   *My ability to do math is. . .*

This prompt can be used at any point in the year to assess students' perceptions of their mathematical ability. Unfortunately, students often equate their ability in math with their behavior as students. If answers indicate that this is the case with your students, you can begin to separate the idea of *ability* from the idea of *behavior.*

Prompt 5   *If I heard someone say "math is fun," I'd say. . .*

This prompt is intended to facilitate a class discussion on the enjoyable aspects of mathematics and to reinforce the idea that students *can* enjoy math.

Prompt 6   *I want to be good at math so that I. . .*

This prompt could be used when talking about how mathematics will lead to later success in college or a career. It may also present an opportunity for you to discuss ability-versus-gender issues with your students. Some researchers believe that one of the reasons boys do better in mathematics than girls is that, from a young age, boys are told—and subsequently believe—that they will need mathematics as they go through school and into careers. Girls are not given the same message and thus do not develop the same belief.

Prompt 7   *When I am in math class, I feel. . .*

Students need to know that they have a right to feel comfortable in mathematics class. By having an opportunity to express their comfort and discomfort, their feelings are validated. Knowing students' feelings will help you to address what is troubling them and to enhance what is positive, and will give you ideas for creating a more comfort-producing environment.

Prompt 8   *In elementary school, math was. . .*

Many of the attitudes students bring to middle school and high school were formed in elementary school. It will probably be evident from reading students' responses to this prompt whether any of them had elementary teachers with math anxiety. On the other hand, some of your students will show you that they had magnificent learning experiences in elementary school, and you will want to continue that positive experience and help them re-create that experience for themselves.

Prompt 9   *My family uses math to. . .*

The home is the first classroom, and it is important for us to understand the perceptions of mathematics that students bring from home. One of the sources of their perceptions is how they see their family members using math—especially whether they see any overt positive uses or any obvious avoidance.

Prompt 10   *If I read your résumé, what would it tell me? What would I learn about your background in mathematics?*

Use this prompt near the beginning of the year, as it is a good way to learn about students' outside interests and will give you insight into difficulties you may want to remedy or successes students have had that you may want to build on. This information will be useful as you plan lessons and discuss applications of mathematics.

Prompt 11   *I am thankful for mathematics. Here are ten reasons why.*

You will want to tuck this holiday-specific prompt into your November lesson plan book. Students may not think they will be able to think of ten reasons, but they will—and don't accept their responses until they do!

Prompt 12   *Mathematics, how do I love thee? Let me count the ways. . .*

Put this prompt into your February lesson plan book. As with Prompt 11, stress that students must come up with ten ways.

Prompt 13   *Mathematics has good points and bad points. Here's what I mean. . .*

Here is a way students can give both sides of their view of mathematics—positive as well as negative. When you read these responses, take special note of the ideas that one student lists as "good points" and another lists as "bad points." This will provide an ideal opportunity for discussion.

Prompt 14   *I study, I pay attention, I take notes, I read my math book, but I still don't get math. Circle T or F, then explain your answer.*

A discussion following or preceding this prompt could address the different kinds of studying that are required to be successful in mathematics.

Prompt 15   *I don't need mathematics. Circle T or F, then explain your answer.*

A dialogue between you and your students about the issues raised by this prompt could focus on areas in life in which a knowledge of mathematics is quite useful—from determining whether your restaurant bill is correct to figuring out how much paint you need to buy to cover all the walls of your room.

Prompt 16   *I will need math in my future. Circle T or F, then explain your answer.*

A discussion about the responses to this prompt could tie into what kinds of mathematics are required in different occupations. You might also discuss consumer situations in which a knowledge of mathematics might be very helpful, such as managing one's finances or making decisions about insurance plans or purchases.

Prompt 17   *Math is my best subject. Circle T or F, then explain your answer.*

This prompt could lead to a discussion about what might make a student like or dislike mathematics and the factors involved in a student's aptitude for the subject.

Prompt 18   *Math doesn't scare me at all. Circle T or F, then explain your answer.*

This prompt could initiate a discussion about students' fears concerning mathematics and ideas about how they might deal with those fears. Math phobia is an obstacle to learning. The source of a student's phobia is often an experience that happened long ago. When you find out the source, you will more likely be able to address it in your class.

Prompt 19   *Math comes easy for me. Circle T or F, then explain your answer.*

This prompt will give you a sense of your students' beliefs about how well they will do in mathematics. A class discussion could yield ideas about what students might do to make mathematics easier.

Prompt 20   *I am looking forward to taking advanced math courses in high school. Circle T or F, then explain your answer.*

Students' responses to this prompt will let you in on how much they know about advanced mathematics and how they feel toward those subjects. Talking with your students about their answers will give you a chance to tell them a bit about high-school mathematics, perhaps offering examples of interesting things that can be done with a knowledge of geometry, algebra, trigonometry, or calculus.

Prompt 21   *I will take advanced math in college. Circle T or F, then explain your answer.*

As with Prompt 20, this prompt will give you insight into your students' ideas about advanced mathematics and offer you a chance to help them with any misconceptions or fears they have about college or advanced mathematics.

Prompt 22   *Mathematics is uncreative. Circle T or F, then explain your answer.*

This prompt will let you know whether your students are bored or excited by mathematics. You might want to talk with them about the more creative aspects of mathematics.

Prompt 23   *Mathematicians can do problems in their heads. Circle T or F, then explain your answer.*

Your students' responses to this prompt will reveal misconceptions they may hold about what it means to do mathematics or to be a mathematician. You might want to talk with them about the many different kinds of work done by people who are called mathematicians.

What does a mathematician look like?

What does a mathematician look like?

Write Starts

***H*mm . . . How does a mathematician think?**

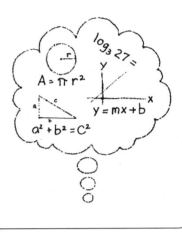

***W*hen will we ever use this stuff?**

My ability to do math is. . .

If I heard someone say "math is fun," I'd say. . .

Write Starts

I want to be good at math so that I. . .

*W*hen I am in math class, I feel. . .

In elementary school, math was. . .

My family uses math to. . .

Write Starts

If I read your résumé, what would it tell me? What would I learn about your background in mathematics?

I am thankful for mathematics. Here are ten reasons why.

Write Starts

Mathematics, how do I love thee? Let me count the ways. . .

Mathematics has good points and bad points. Here's what I mean. . .

I study, I pay attention, I take notes, I read my math book, but I still don't get math. Circle T or F, then explain your answer.

I don't need mathematics. Circle T or F, then explain your answer.

Write Starts

I will need math in my future. Circle T or F, then explain your answer.

Math is my best subject. Circle T or F, then explain your answer.

Math doesn't scare me at all. Circle T or F, then explain your answer.

Math comes easy for me. Circle T or F, then explain your answer.

Write Starts

I am looking forward to taking advanced math courses in high school. Circle T or F, then explain your answer.

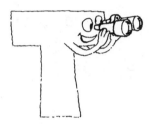  

I will take advanced math in college. Circle T or F, then explain your answer.

Mathematics is uncreative. Circle T or F, then explain your answer.

Mathematicians can do problems in their heads. Circle T or F, then explain your answer.

Write Starts

2

Succeeding in the Mathematics Classroom

This section focuses on the tools and strategies students need to learn and succeed in the mathematics classroom. These prompts emphasize the idea that math is not a spectator sport. You can use them as an entree to a discussion about expectations for preparedness in your class, and as a springboard for a schoolwide push for teaching students how to learn and succeed across the content areas. Teachers in all subject areas can work together so that students not only learn—but learn how to learn.

Prompt 24   *To do my work in mathematics, I will need these tools:*

This prompt is intended to follow an explanation of what you expect students to bring to class. You may want to write your list on the master before photocopying it for students. Their job will be to explain why they will need each item and what they will do with it.

Prompt 25   *In math, we always work in pencil. What are the pros and cons of this convention?*

As mathematics teachers, we often hear, "Why do we have to do this in pencil?" You can sidestep this comment by starting right out with this prompt. Simply state it as fact— *In mathematics we work in pencil*—and offer this prompt to give students their first and last opportunity of the year to argue against pencils.

Prompt 26   *How do you take notes for this class?*

Many students have no method for taking notes in mathematics classes. They are usually so busy writing down everything you are writing on the board that they pay little attention to what you are saying. If you use this prompt early in the year, give the following directions along with it: "I am going to compile your responses to this question into a master list and share it with the whole class. Please take the time to think about the special methods you use to take notes in mathematics. If you can't think of anything, explain what you have tried that has not worked." The prompt will bring some good suggestions that can be shared with the class, and you will get information about where students' note-taking weaknesses lie to help you plan lessons that incorporate note taking.

Prompt 27   *What are some of the special ways that you read your math book?*

Many students have no method for reading mathematics. If they even consider reading math, they try the same techniques they use in English or history—and these are usually not applicable. Left-to-right, top-to-bottom reading is just not appropriate for math. If you use this prompt early in the year, give the following directions along with it: "I am going to compile your responses to this question into a master list and share it with the whole class. Please take the time to think about the special ways that you read in mathematics. If you can't think of anything, explain what you have tried that has not worked." The prompt will bring some good suggestions that can be shared with the class, and you will get information about where students' reading weaknesses lie to help you plan lessons that incorporate reading strategies.

Prompt 28   *Picture yourself doing math. Describe what you see.*

Athletes often use imaging as part of their training. Speakers imagine themselves receiving a standing ovation at the end of a speech. Actors envision themselves hitting their cues with perfect timing. Students can employ this powerful technique as well, imagining themselves in successful situations and then expecting that their performance will match their image. You may want to write similar prompts that ask students to picture themselves taking a test and being confident while doing so, or to picture themselves successfully completing their homework in a quiet setting.

Prompt 29   *Computers help me learn math. Here's how.*

The NCTM *Standards* recommend that developing computation skills includes learning to use appropriate technology. The computer is one of many technological tools students can use to learn mathematics. Most students have had some experience with computers, but it may not have been in mathematics. This prompt will lead well into a lesson or unit on computers. It could also be used as a closure activity for such a lesson or unit.

Prompt 30   *How my calculator helps me with math. . . What else I wish my calculator could do:*

One of the assumptions of the authors of the NCTM *Standards* is that "all students will have a calculator." In high school, it is assumed that "scientific calculators with graphing capabilities will be available to all students at all times." This prompt can be given several times over the year as students learn different aspects and applications of their calculators.

To do my work in mathematics, I will need these tools:

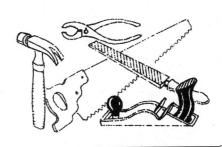

In math, we always work in pencil. What are the pros and cons of this convention?

Pros   Cons

How do you take notes for this class?

What are some of the special ways that you read your math book?

Picture yourself doing math. Describe what you see.

Computers help me learn math. Here's how.

How my calculator helps me with math:

What else I wish my calculator could do:

MAY I HELP YOU?

Write Starts

3

Doing Homework

Doing homework is essential for learning mathematics. There is no way around having students work at home, practicing their computation and problem-solving skills.

You can use these prompts to facilitate in-class discussion about homework—its purpose, its secrets, its necessity. The responses to most of them are intended to be shared with other members of the class. Students who are successful with their homework can share insights—insights that you could also share, but that might not be heard from you— with other students. Plan to make these prompts part of your class on a regular basis.

Prompt 31   *What do you do when you get stuck on your homework?*

Successful students have a plan for what to do when they encounter a problem with their homework. The responses to this prompt will give you a good handle on which students are likely to be successful because they already have strategies at their disposal and which students could benefit from ideas on what to do when they are stuck.

Prompt 32   *The toughest math problem I figured out on last night's homework was _____ , and this is what made it so tough.*

This prompt has students assess their homework problems in terms of difficulty level and gives them a chance to revel in the fact that they conquered a difficult problem. As students reflect on the difficulty levels of problems they have competed, they gain an awareness of and learn to estimate the task demands of upcoming assignments— and acknowledge that problems that take up more space in the book may not be the hardest problems. It also makes them consider the idea that on nearly all homework assignments, some problems will be relatively easy, some will be of medium difficulty, and some will be more difficult. Research indicates that strategic learners are able to gauge the task demands of each learning situation. This prompt, and others like it, will help lead students and teachers to an understanding of the task demands.

Prompt 33   *What is the key to understanding tonight's homework?*

This prompt can be valuable when you have taught a new concept that must be applied in order for students to complete their homework. By writing out the "key" or concept you have been teaching, they will be more likely to carry the idea home with them.

Prompt 34   *When I'm doing my homework, it would be great if my computer could help me. Here's what I would ask. . .*

To formulate a response to this question, students will have to identify the specific area in which they would like help. This will help them to formulate better questions to ask you the next day when you ask, "Are there any questions on last night's homework?"

Prompt 35   *I think I am right on target with the way I answered this homework problem. Let me explain.*

When students explain their reasoning in writing, it can be examined by others and by themselves and reveal logical or illogical processes. This prompt can be used frequently. You may want to make multiple copies of this prompt for students to keep in their notebooks to use whenever it is appropriate.

Prompt 36   *I know I've been "dragon" my feet on getting this assignment in. At last, here it is—and here's why it took me so long.*

This prompt is quite useful because it will prevent you from having to listen to long excuses about why homework is late or why it will be late. Let students know that they are to answer this prompt whenever they turn in an assignment late. Their explanations may not prevent them from losing points, but occasionally they will be valid, and you will often learn from what your students have written.

What do you do when you get stuck on your homework?

*T*he toughest math problem I figured out on last night's homework was _____ , and this is what made it so tough.

Write Starts

What is the key to understanding tonight's homework?

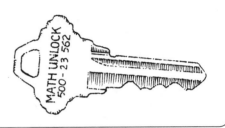

Prompt **33**

When I'm doing my homework, it would be great if my computer could help me. Here's what I would ask. . .

Prompt **34**

Write Starts

I think I am right on target with the way I answered this homework problem. Let me explain.

I know I've been "dragon" my feet on getting this assignment in. At last, here it is—and here's why it took me so long.

Write Starts

4

Focusing on Today's Learning

One of our favorite "Family Circus" cartoons shows the parents asking the children at the dinner table about what they learned at school that day. In turn, the children say, "Nothing," "Not much," etc. The father says, "Great. Then you can go out and get jobs tomorrow." Immediately, the children begin to relate all the different facts and ideas they encountered that day.

Children and young adults are seldom asked to discuss or to rejoice in their learning. The writing prompts in this section are meant to pay tribute to a student's new learning. We recommend that you make these prompts available to students and remind students of them often. We have noticed that when we first use one of these, students give us the "What the. . . ?" look. It is sad that many have not been asked what they have learned, nor to celebrate it. After a while, students ask if they can do one of the "I know it" prompts.

Students' responses to these prompts are valuable for sharing with parents and administrators to demonstrate that your students are learning. We believe that having students notice and take pride in their learning is a key to success in mathematics.

Prompt 37 *I've had an explosion of knowledge regarding. . .*

This prompt can expose interesting but private experiences students have had about what they are learning, and it offers them a platform on which to talk about their insights freely.

Prompt 38 *I'm cheering about what I learned today!*

This prompt is a bit corny, but it works. When a certain level of rapport has been established in your classroom, you can have students share their answers to this prompt.

Prompt 39 *After today's lesson, what do you feel you have mastered?*

We like using this prompt on an individual basis more than as a whole-class prompt, because there are days when a student feels he or she has not mastered anything—and we don't want the "nothing" answer.

Prompt 40   *What did you learn today that you didn't already know?*

This is a good prompt for providing closure on the day's lesson. If the answer to this one is "nothing," you might also give students a prompt that asks about when they did learn the information that was presented in class or why they disagree with the information shared in class. Students will learn there's always something to write about—there's a prompt for every occasion!

Prompt 41   *After today's learning activity, I'll tell you what I notice.*

This is a good prompt to use when you have presented a lesson that was intended to provide an *aha!* experience.

Prompt 42   *NOW I get it!*

One of the best aspects of teaching mathematics is the look of "Oh, yeah, now I get it!" on students' faces. As soon as you see this look, get out this prompt!

Prompt 43   *"Wooden" you know?! I learned something today!*

This is corny, but it's a fun prompt for teasing students—in a positive way, of course!

Prompt 44   *I'd like to shine a spotlight on what I've just learned, which is this:*

This prompt gives students the opportunity to show off their new learning over a day, a week, or a unit. Their responses would make a good display for a bulletin board with a big spotlight on it—or even for a wall with a real spotlight shining on it!

Prompt 45   *I don't want to forget what I learned today.*

Use this prompt to help reinforce the learning that has occurred on a specific day.

I*'ve had an explosion of knowledge regarding...*

I'm cheering about what I learned today!

After today's lesson, what do you feel you have mastered?

Write Starts

What did you learn today that you didn't already know?

After today's learning activity, I'll tell you what I notice.

NOW I get it!

*"**W**ooden"* you know?! I learned something today!

*Write **S**tarts*

I'd like to shine a spotlight on what I've just learned, which is this:

I don't want to forget what I learned today.

Write Starts

5

Asking Questions

The peer pressure against asking questions or appearing interested in class is staggering. Although we all work to change this attitude, it remains in some classrooms despite our best efforts. Whether or not this pressure exists in your classroom, assigning these writing prompts will produce positive responses. They allow students to ask questions, express confusion, or invite help—privately.

Have copies of each of the prompts in this section available in the classroom at all times for students to use. For students who don't like to ask questions in class, writing out their questions—to be read by you—allows them to get their questions answered. You may also want to give students a copy of one or more of these prompts to keep in a designated section of their notebooks.

For these writing assignments to be effective, you need to respond to them. You may choose to respond individually to a student's question or to address it in class.

Prompt 46   *I have a few questions about what we're doing in here.*

This prompt will help students sort out what they do and don't understand about what they are learning.

Prompt 47   *I have a question. . .*

This is a useful prompt for students who shy away from asking questions in class.

Prompt 48   *I was just wondering. . .*

This prompt can encourage students who want to expand on an idea they encountered in or out of class.

Prompt 49   *Help! I need more of an explanation for. . .*

This prompt will help students target processes, procedures, or concepts they don't quite understand.

Prompt 50   *I am still puzzled over. . .*

This prompt can be helpful for students who feel everybody else understands something they don't. Their answers will let you know when it would be helpful to explain a concept in a new way.

Prompt 51   *This does not compute. Show me where I'm malfunctioning.*

You may want to have students respond to this prompt when they are having trouble with a specific homework problem.

I have a few questions about what we're doing in here.

I have a question. . .

I was just wondering. . .

*H*elp! I need more of an explanation for. . .

Write Starts

I am still puzzled over. . .

This does not compute. Show me where I'm malfunctioning.

Write Starts

6

Revising Ideas and Relearning

Trying new ideas and making mistakes are important parts of learning mathematics. However, many people are afraid of making mistakes. The underlying message of the writing prompts in this section is that mistakes are fine and should be used to further thinking and learning. Be sure to complete some of these yourself to share with students. Modeling often says much more than lecturing!

Prompt 52   *What's the error in this problem?*

The ability to recognize errors and to explain them is an important skill in mathematics. Students sometimes resist checking their work for errors. You might want to pull a problem—with an error in its solution—from a student's homework to put on the "chalkboard" of the prompt. We recommend using this prompt often and giving many students a turn at having a problem on the chalkboard.

Prompt 53   *OOPS! Let me tell you about the error I made on one of my homework problems.*

This prompt brings a bit of fun into the request that students go back to their homework to look for errors and to rethink the process that resulted in an error.

Prompt 54   *Is there any value in making mistakes in math? Circle Y or N to indicate your feelings about this question, then explain your answer.*

We believe it is important for students to appreciate the value of mistakes. After students have answered this prompt, you might have them do a "Line Up" based on the strength of their answers. Have students line up in order of their opinions. Students will need to discuss and debate to determine who has the strongest *yes* response, the next strongest *yes* response, down to the strongest *no* response. This kinesthetic activity is useful for students who have been sitting a little too long and need to move.

Prompt 55   *What are the pros and cons of making errors?*

Listing-type prompts such as this one engage the competitive spirit—who can come up with the most pros and the most cons—and encourage deeper thinking than may otherwise result.

Prompt 56   *Here are some ideas I once had about math, but now I realize they belong in the trash.*

This prompt, given a couple of months into the school year, can encourage a lot of thinking. It gives students time to learn and to rethink some of their previously held ideas, and students' answers can be quite gratifying for you to read.

Prompt 57   *What did you learn today that goes against what you already know or believe?*

This prompt taps into higher-level thinking by asking students to reflect on what seems *counterintuitive* to them. You might even want to use the word *counterintuitive* with your students when you discuss the question—it just sounds interesting!

What's the error in this problem?

OOPS! Let me tell you about the error I made on one of my homework problems.

Is there any value in making mistakes in math? Circle Y or N to indicate your feelings about this question, then explain your answer.

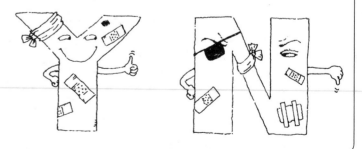

What are the pros and cons of making errors?

Pros	Cons

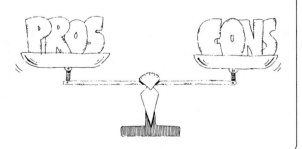

Here are some ideas I once had about math, but now I realize they belong in the trash.

What did you learn today that goes against what you already know or believe?

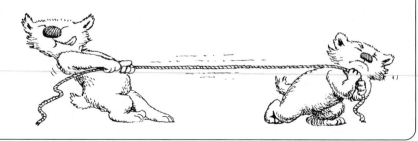

7

Connecting New and Old Information

The writing prompts in this section serve two purposes: they reinforce the concept that learning involves connecting the new to the known, and they serve as a response to students who say, "I already know that" or "We learned that last year." These prompts also give students a chance to celebrate what they already know.

Prompt 58   *What did you learn today that reinforces what you already know or believe?*

This prompt is useful as a closure activity. Offer it as one of several that students can choose from, because not everyone will have an answer to this prompt every day.

Prompt 59   *What served as a review for you today?*

This is a wonderful prompt to use when you hear, "Ms. Teacher, I already know that!" Just respond, "Super. Then tell me how what we did was a review for you."

Prompt 60   *To solve this problem, I had to. . .*

Integral to mathematics is the idea of building upon previous knowledge. You can help support that concept through prompts such as this one, which requires that students think back to what they have already learned and to analyze how it integrates with what they are currently exploring.

Prompt 61   *Here's what I now know that I didn't know on the first day I walked in here.*

This is an affirming prompt to use on a day when you need your spirits lifted: the answers will make you feel better about the good job you are doing. Students write about *aha!* experiences they have had, words they now understand, and concepts that have become clear since being in your class.

Prompt 62   *A cornucopia of learning has occurred for me so far this year in math.*

You may want to use this prompt around the Thanksgiving holiday. Tell students that you are sure their minds are overflowing with information, just as the cornucopia overflows.

Prompt 63   *Here are some things from this chapter that I better file away because I will need them in upcoming chapters.*

It is essential to reinforce the notion that everything students learn in mathematics serves as a foundation for everything they will learn. You can offer this prompt at the end of each chapter and have students review their responses often to see if they correctly anticipated what concepts would be built on in future chapters.

Prompt 64   *Well, I'm packing it in for this year. Here's what I'm taking with me for next year.*

You can use this as an end-of-year or end-of-semester prompt. Give it to students as a take-home assignment, asking them to go through their notes, notebooks, and books to review for themselves what they have learned, and then to decide what will be the most valuable. Having them justify their answers is quite useful, too.

What did you learn today that reinforces what you already know or believe?

What served as a review for you today?

To solve this problem, I had to. . .

Here's what I now know that I didn't know on the first day I walked in here.

Write Starts

A cornucopia of learning has occurred for me so far this year in math.

Here are some things from this chapter that I better file away because I will need them in upcoming chapters.

Well, I'm packing it in for this year. Here's what I'm taking with me for next year.

Write Starts

8

Relating Mathematics
to Other Subjects

Many schools are moving toward a more interdisciplinary approach to learning in an effort to demonstrate to students the interrelated nature of the content areas. Instead of keeping content areas cordoned off from one another, many educators are working to make the distinctions fuzzier and to allow students to see the connections between subjects.

These writing prompts ask students to think about the relationships between mathematics and other subjects and between mathematics and life outside the classroom. You may want to share these prompts with teachers of other subjects, who could create similar prompts about how their subject connects with mathematics or other content areas.

Prompt 65   *What is a real-life application or example of something you learned today?*

Put this question to students rather than waiting for them to ask you, "When are we ever going to need this?" Thinking of answers may not be easy initially, but after they have been asked this question several times, they will anticipate it. Students will automatically begin to search for places outside the classroom where what they are learning is being applied.

Prompt 66   *People in the communications field use math in these ways:*

You might use this prompt prior to or as a follow-up to taking a field trip or having a guest speaker talk to the class about how he or she uses mathematics.

Prompt 67   *Here's how what I am learning in math branches off into my other classes:*

You could use this prompt as part of an interdisciplinary unit or just as a way of encouraging students to focus on how mathematics relates to other subjects. Encourage students to think broadly as they respond. For example, ask them to consider the thinking strategies they are learning, the problem-solving behaviors they are perfecting, or the study skills they have recently gained.

Prompt 68   *What kinds of mathematics did ship captains use to travel across vast oceans 500 years ago? What kinds of mathematics do ship captains use today?*

This approach encourages students to think about how mathematics is used—and has been used—in many fields and for many types of problem solving.

Prompt 69   *How is math used in your favorite sport?*

Many students have a favorite sport, and analyzing how mathematics is used in that sport could be a nice tie-in with the work they are doing in class. Since not everyone has a favorite sport, you could offer this prompt as a choice along with some of the others in this section.

Prompt 70   *Write about this idea: Home is where the heart is—and home is where the math is.*

Students need to know that they will use mathematics for the rest of their lives, both in their work and in their homes. You could use this prompt as an opening for such a discussion.

Prompt 71   *Write about as many ways as you can think of that math and science are related.*

Mathematics and science are inseparable. It is worthwhile to have students respond to this prompt in your class—and to have their science teachers ask them to respond to it in science class. Compare and contrast the answers; given that only the setting of the request is different, the responses will be quite interesting.

Prompt 72   *What kind of math is used in art?*

This prompt may appeal to students who constantly sketch or doodle. You can create other prompts of this type for every content area and career field.

Prompt 73   *Here's how what we are learning connects to life outside the classroom.*

You can use this prompt several times during the year to reinforce the connections between mathematics and the rest of life.

What is a real-life application or example of something you learned today?

People in the communications field use math in these ways:

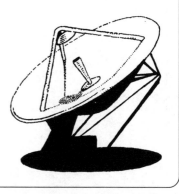

*H*ere's how what I am learning in math branches off into my other classes:

*W*hat kinds of mathematics did ship captains use to travel across vast oceans 500 years ago? What kinds of mathematics do ship captains use today?

How is math used in your favorite sport?

Write about this idea: Home is where the heart is—and home is where the math is.

Write about as many ways as you can think of that math and science are related.

What kind of math is used in art?

Here's how what we are learning connects to life outside the classroom.

Write Starts

9

Taking Responsibility for Behavior and Performance

The writing prompts in this section allow students to focus on their own behavior and give you and your students an opportunity to have written conversations about their behavior and performance. We believe that students need to take responsibility for their own behavior and learning. The prompts also help facilitate discussions between students and teachers and students, teachers, and parents. You will probably want to use these prompts over and over throughout the year.

Prompt 74   *I know I'm in the doghouse because of the way I've acted in class lately. Here's my plan for how I'm going to turn my behavior around.*

By the time students are in middle school and high school, they should be cognizant of their behavior—both good and bad—and what it takes to have the former. This prompt— for individual use and to be shared only with you—can open communication between you and certain students.

Prompt 75   *Here's an explanation for why my grade is going down in this class.*

This prompt can be used as needed during grading periods, perhaps about the time progress reports are made. With students' permission, you might want to include the prompt with the progress report sent to their homes.

Prompt 76   *Here's an explanation for why my grade is going up in this class.*

As with Prompt 75, this prompt can be used during grading periods and perhaps sent home with progress reports.

Prompt 77   *On the final day of this unit, here's what I know and here's what I think of my performance throughout the unit.*

Students are often quite honest and forthcoming on prompts such as this one. This is a private communication between you and a student and provides a fair amount of insight into the student's performance.

Prompt 78   *In evaluating my performance this semester, here's what I have to say.*

As with Prompt 77, this prompt can open the doors for honest communication between student and teacher.

I know I'm in the doghouse because of the way I've acted in class lately. Here's my plan for how I'm going to turn my behavior around.

Here's an explanation for why my grade is going down in this class.

Here's an explanation for why my grade is going up in this class.

Write Starts

On the final day of this unit, here's what I know and here's what I think of my performance throughout the unit.

In evaluating my performance this semester, here's what I have to say.

Write Starts

10

Evaluating the Learning Environment

The writing prompts in this section give you and your students an opportunity to communicate openly about the classroom learning environment. The majority of these prompts create an expectation of a positive response. Some of them open the door for students to respond to something they perceive as negative, but do so in a positive way. Our experience shows us that when students are given a chance to be heard, the situation can be addressed with minimum disturbance. The result is often an improved learning environment for all.

You too can share your excitement or displeasure about something in the learning environment by responding to a prompt from this section. Share your response with your students by reading it, posting it, or displaying it on the overhead projector.

Prompt 79   *I'm having a great time in math and I'd like to tell you about it!*

This prompt provides an opportunity for students to express a positive response to the classroom learning environment. It helps set a positive tone in class and lets students know that you expect and want them to be enjoying the experience.

Prompt 80   *Today, I really thought something was a turkey of an idea. Let me tell you what it was—and why I didn't care for it.*

Even though we generally believe our classes go well and meet the needs of our students, we are experienced enough to know that sometimes we do something that is perceived by one or more students as a less-than-wonderful idea. Making this prompt available to students to use it when (and if) they think necessary lets them know you are open to their viewpoint. You might also request that students offer suggestions for improvement.

Prompt 81   *I am just sick of. . .*

This somewhat negatively phrased prompt has provided us with valuable insights over the years. Students appreciate having an opportunity to express themselves in this way. There are times that we continue to use something we think is working—until our students are ready to skewer us. It is not always our teaching that they are tired of; for example, students may be frustrated because one student dominates the class or because the class is frequently interrupted by announcements. When a student takes the time to respond to this prompt (keep copies of it available), you will know it is time to rethink certain plans, activities, or classroom structures.

Prompt 82   *I don't think I am the only one thinking this. . .*

Middle-school and high-school students are sometimes reluctant to express themselves in front of the class. This prompt gives individuals a chance to tell you something— a compliment, a request, a complaint—they might not be able to otherwise.

Prompt 83   *What do you hope we talk more about tomorrow or some other day soon?*

This prompt will likely generate many fresh ideas about what your students would like to learn. Students may have an issue related to the school or the class that they want to talk about, and you can take five minutes at the end of class to address it. We have found that, especially with teenagers, you might as well address their concerns on your terms, because otherwise they will force the issue on theirs.

Prompt 84   *It's time I let you know all the things I like about this class and the way it is structured.*

You might choose to use this "warm fuzzy" prompt on a "cold prickly" day when you could use some encouragement, or just have it available for students to use any time they see fit.

Prompt 85   *Upcoming features I would like to see in this class:*

Students often give ideas for lessons, units, and directions to go in when they respond to this prompt. Your asking this question gives them a sense that they have a say in the classroom and the learning that goes on within it. Let them know that legitimate, well-thought-out suggestions are valued and are more likely to be implemented than silly, unreasonable responses (though you will probably still receive a few of the latter).

Prompt 86   *What can you tell your friends about what you are learning in this class?*

This prompt is a variation on the theme of assuming that students are learning and asking them to tell you about it.

Prompt 87   *What I missed most about our class was this:*

This prompt is intended to be used following a holiday or break. You may want to fill this one out and share it with your students, just as you are asking them to share their thoughts with you.

Prompt 88   *The biggest surprise to me in this class is. . .*

This is a very good way to bring closure to the year. We never know what will strike students as surprising in our classes. Sometimes students focus on classroom climate, sometimes the text, sometimes the humor, sometimes the fact that they actually *like* math.

I'm having a great time in math and I'd like to tell you about it!

*T*oday, I really thought something was a turkey of an idea. Let me tell you what it was—and why I didn't care for it.

Write Starts

I am just sick of. . .

I don't think I am the only one thinking this. . .

Write Starts

What do you hope we talk more about tomorrow or some other day soon?

It's time I let you know all the things I like about this class and the way it is structured.

Upcoming features I would like to see in this class:

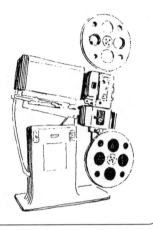

What can you tell your friends about what you are learning in this class?

What I missed most about our class was this:

The biggest surprise to me in this class is. . .

Write Starts

11

Solving Problems

Problem solving is at the heart of mathematics. A broad range of problem-solving experiences—including having students work on complex problems, in small cooperative groups and with the whole class, and on open-ended problems with no right answer—is supported by the NCTM *Standards* and by literature in critical and creative thinking. The writing prompts in this section encourage students to reflect on their problem-solving ability and to demonstrate their understanding of what good problem solvers do. Discuss students' responses to these prompts in small groups or as a class. Many of these prompts are great to use as class openers.

Prompt 89 *Good problem solvers do four things:*

- *They read the problem.*
- *They devise a plan for solving the problem.*
- *They carry out their plan.*
- *They check their work.*

Evaluate your problem-solving ability based on each of these four behaviors.

Students often get stuck on their homework and have no idea how to get unstuck. Use this prompt, which is based on George Polya's idea about good problem solvers, to remind your students what "good" problem solvers do and to help them evaluate their own problem-solving methods.

Prompt 90 *An algorithm is a sequence of steps that leads to a desired result. Write an algorithm for a task you want to accomplish.*

Your students must remember many algorithms to complete their assignments successfully. This prompt asks students to write their own algorithm for doing a specific task that they choose. After students have answered this prompt, have them exchange prompts with a partner and do exactly what their partner's prompt says. Hold a discussion centering on these questions: Did each student accomplish the task that his or her partner wanted? Why or why not? What happens when we don't follow all the steps of a mathematical algorithm? Have them answer the prompt again, only this time stipulating that the task they want to accomplish be a mathematical task.

Prompt 91   *"Trial and error is a viable problem-solving strategy." Circle Y or N to indicate your feelings about this statement, then explain your answer.*

Students may either agree or disagree with this statement—we hope they agree, since we know it to be true—as long as they justify their response. Students can learn from their mistakes, especially if they have some sort of method to their mathematics. Use this prompt to remind them that when all else fails, try guessing and checking!

Prompt 92   *One sign of a good problem solver is. . .*

This prompt should serve as a reminder to students and help keep them on the problem-solving highway. In talking about the answers to this prompt, students should realize that people are not born good problem solvers, but that good problem solvers have learned and remembered to do certain things—things all students can learn to do when they are faced with a problem.

Prompt 93   *Don't forget to remember that when you. . . you must. . .*

Use this prompt to help students remember all the steps of an important process; for example, they might write: Don't forget to remember that when you add fractions, you must first have common denominators. You can either supply the first insert and have students write about what they have to remember, or students can decide what they are having a difficult time remembering and fill in both parts for themselves.

Prompt 94   *I have an easier way to solve this problem! Here's what I did. . .*

Students often find good shortcuts for problems. Those shortcuts become more powerful if the students understand why they work.

Prompt 95   *Let me tell you about a problem that was very hard.*

This prompt asks students to think about what made a particularly hard problem difficult—such as the language of the problem, the student's unfamiliarity with the wording of the problem, the problem's requirement that the student use more than one skill, a certain skill required for the problem that is a weak area for the student, or a lengthy problem that intimidated the student into thinking the problem was hard. When students can examine what makes a problem seem difficult, they are on their way to making that type of problem easier.

Good problem solvers do four things:

- They read the problem.
- They devise a plan for solving the problem.
- They carry out their plan.
- They check their work.

Evaluate your problem-solving ability based on each of these four behaviors.

An algorithm is a sequence of steps that leads to a desired result.
Write an algorithm for a task you want to accomplish.

"Trial and error is a viable problem-solving strategy."
Circle Y or N to indicate your feelings about this statement,
then explain your answer.

Write Starts

One sign of a good problem solver is. . .

Don't forget to remember that when you . . .

you must. . .

I have an easier way to solve this problem? Here's what I did. . .

---

*L*et me tell you about a problem that was very hard.

Write Starts

12

Writing Your Own Math Prompts

We hope this section will inspire you to create your own writing prompts. The possibilities are endless for using writing as a way for students to demonstrate their knowledge and learning—as well as for students to use writing to learn.

To create your own writing prompts, start by listing some possible writing formats, and then create writing assignments that employ each format. Here are just a few types of writing formats and how they could be assigned.

- Write an *advice column* for your fellow math students.
- Suggest an *alternative to counting sheep* for someone who can't sleep, such as counting prime numbers.
- Write an *analogy* that describes the relationship between factoring and multiplying binomials.
- Provide the *address* of the vertex angle in an isosceles triangle.
- Write an *anecdote* about the number pi.

Have fun coming up with writing assignments—and offering your students some variety!

Prompt 96   *Write a word problem.*

You can use this prompt during almost any unit of study. Encourage students to write real word problems, not the type that have little application to real life. You may enjoy having students challenge each other with their word problems.

Prompt 97   *Rewrite one of your homework problems in English, without using mathematical symbols.*

To translate symbols to English or English to symbols, students must have a reasonable understanding of the concepts being represented. This prompt reinforces the meaning of the symbols and is really enjoyed by students who are linguistically strong but sometimes feel less adequate mathematically.

Prompt 98   *Write a script for the message your favorite mathematician might leave on his or her answering machine.*

Learning about the history of mathematics, including the people who are the history-makers, is part of many mathematics curricula. A prompt such as this one gives students a fun way to show what they have learned about a particular mathematician. Completed sets of these responses may be more stimulating and enjoyable to read than reports on mathematicians!

Prompt 99   *Write a letter to your favorite mathematician—or write a letter you wish your favorite mathematician would write to you.*

Similar to Prompt 98, this prompt offers a creative way for students to demonstrate what they have learned in their study of a particular mathematician.

Prompt 100   *Explain it to me.*

This is a fairly generic prompt that you can have students respond to after doing a word problem, completing a proof, generating hypotheses about something, and the like. Modeling how to give a verbal explanation of a mathematical task before expecting students to do the same would be valuable.

Prompt 101   *How would you sell math?*

You might enjoy having students complete this prompt early in the year and then again later, looking for changes in their "selling points." It is a good measure of how students' attitudes about mathematics are developing. (You could substitute the topic *geometry*, *linear algebra*, *precalculus*, or whatever is appropriate.)

Write a word problem.

Rewrite one of your homework problems in English, without using mathematical symbols.

Write a script for the message your favorite mathematician might leave on his or her answering machine.

Write Starts

Write a letter to your favorite mathematician—or write a letter you wish your favorite mathematician would write to you.

Explain it to me.

How would you sell math?

Write Starts

References

Geeslin, William E. "Using Writing About Mathematics as a Teaching Technique," *Mathematics Teacher* 70 (Feb. 1977): 112–15.

National Council of Teachers of Mathematics. *Curriculum and Evaluation Standards for School Mathematics.* Reston, Va.: NCTM, 1989.